GCSE Grade Booster:
A* Chemistry

Dr Andrew Grevatt

Badger Learning
Oldmedow Road
Hardwick Industrial Estate
Kings Lynn
PE30 4JJ

Tel: 01438 791037
Fax: 01438 791036

GCSE Grade Booster: A* Chemistry Teacher Book & CD
ISBN 978 1 78147 440 2

Note: due to the nature of the internet, it is vital that you check web links before they are used in the classroom.

Publisher: Susan Ross
Designer: Sarah Channing-Wright & Cambridge Publishing Management Limited
Cover Designer: Adam Wilmott
Illustrator: Tim Oliver
Cover Photo: Alamy
Typesetting and project management: Cambridge Publishing Management Limited

Printed in the UK

Contents

Experiment Boosters

Argument Boosters

References

Contents on CD

All of the Boosters are available on the CD.

Editable content

Editable Boosters are included for teachers and students to make their own tasks based on their examination specification. They are:

- Knowledge Booster 5: Create a Knowledge Booster
- Concept Booster 5a: Create a Concept Booster
- Experiment Booster 1a: Explaining Experiments
- Experiment Booster 1b: Explaining Experiments Support Sheet
- Experiment Booster 5: Understanding Graphs and Charts
- Argument Booster 5: Controversial Issues

Introduction

The importance of an A* grade in science or chemistry cannot be underestimated. Learners who leave school with at least an A grade in science or chemistry have far more opportunities open to them, particularly going on to A-levels and beyond. Anything that teachers can do to support learners in achieving this grade should be done.

This book is a collection of activities that aim to improve learners' knowledge, understanding and confidence to achieve at least a grade A. These activities could be used as part of intervention lessons, homework activities with class work follow-up, within lessons as part of a scheme of work, or for focused revision sessions.

These activities have been developed by consulting the examiners' reports from the past five years and prioritising the most common mistakes in learners' responses to examination questions. The focus of the tasks is on the knowledge, understanding and skills required for the 'higher' questions (up to grade A*), each with a focus on the most common mistakes.

As with all teaching resources, how the teacher integrates the resource into their teaching is essential to their success. Motivated learners may be able to take these tasks home, try them and improve their own knowledge, understanding, skills and confidence. However, on the whole, teachers need to use their motivational skills to engage learners with the resource and provide effective feedback. Each activity has notes for teachers with guidance and ideas.

I have thought carefully about the selection and design of these tasks. I hope that you find them a useful addition to your teaching resources.

Andrew Grevatt

About the Author

Andrew is the author of the popular Badger Science Assessment for Learning Key Stage 3 and 4 resources. He completed his doctorate in the Use and Impact of Levelled Assessment Tasks in Science Education in 2010. He has a research interest in progression in learning. He was an Advanced Skills Teacher in secondary science. He is currently a teaching and research fellow at the University of Sussex and an international education advisor, specialising in school based assessment.

Acknowledgements

I dedicate this publication to Geoffrey, who has bravely retaken his science GCSEs at the age of 35. Fingers crossed for an A!

Many people have influenced my ideas and the development of these tasks. First, the excellent and enthusiastic teachers with whom I have had the privilege to work, face-to-face or via social media, particularly Twitter. Second, my colleagues, who engage and challenge me with the practice, policy and theory of teaching and learning. Third, my family who support all my endeavours. Finally, all those at Badger Learning who believe in my writing and ideas, and help me make an impact in classrooms around the country.

Introduction

What Does an A* Grade in Chemistry Look Like?

The Grade Descriptors published by GCSE examination specifications can be analysed to help understand what knowledge, understanding and skills are expected for achieving an A grade.

The Grade Descriptor states that candidates should: 'demonstrate a detailed knowledge and understanding of science content and how science works, encompassing the principal concepts, techniques, and facts across all areas of the specification'.

Knowledge

- Knowledge of technical vocabulary and techniques, and use these appropriately.

- Describe how, and why, decisions about uses of science are made in contexts familiar to them, and apply this knowledge to unfamiliar situations.

- Use this knowledge, together with information from other sources, to help plan a scientific task, such as: a practical procedure, testing an idea, answering a question, or solving a problem.

Understanding

- A good understanding of the relationships between data, evidence, and scientific explanations and theories.

- Awareness of areas of uncertainty in scientific knowledge and ability to explain how scientific theories can be changed by new evidence.

- Demonstrate good understanding of the benefits and risks of scientific advances, and identify ethical issues related to these.

Skills

- Clearly demonstrate communication and numerical skills appropriate to a range of situations.

- Demonstrate a good understanding of the relationships between data, evidence, and scientific explanations and theories.

- Choose appropriate methods for collecting first-hand and secondary data, interpret and question data skilfully, and evaluate the methods used.

- Carry out a range of practical tasks safely and skilfully, selecting and using equipment appropriately to make relevant and precise observations.

- Select a method of presenting data appropriate to the task.

- Draw and justify conclusions consistent with the evidence collected, and suggest improvements to the methods used that would enable them to collect more valid and reliable evidence.

How the Tasks Have Been Developed

These tasks have been designed by building on a combination of what we know about the common difficulties faced by learners doing 'higher' questions in examinations within a framework based on learning theories.

The theoretical framework is based on Bloom's Taxonomy of Educational Objectives. If you look at the Grade Descriptors for grade A, you will find that they fit within the 'Synthesis' and 'Evaluation' parts of Bloom's Taxonomy. In fact, in the broadest sense, examination grades can be correlated with Bloom's taxonomy domains.

Bloom's Cognitive Domain	Examination Grades	Simple Descriptors
Synthesis	A*	Synthesise
Evaluation	A	Evaluate
Analysis	B	Analyse
Application	C	Explain
Comprehension	D	Describe
Knowledge	E	Identify

The tasks in this book have been developed using these principles. Learners who have excellent knowledge and comprehension and are able to apply these in unfamiliar situations are likely to achieve at least an A grade.

So, these tasks have been designed to build extensive knowledge and comprehension, and to develop the skills of analysis, evaluation and synthesis for GCSE science. The Knowledge Boosters support widening knowledge and comprehension; they will increase learners' confidence in the keywords and definitions. The Concept Boosters build on that knowledge and comprehension to encourage application of knowledge and understanding; they can be used as a task on their own or followed by the exam-style questions that are of increasing demand – Explain, Apply and Evaluate. The Experiment Boosters encourage analysis of experiments, highlighting common issues and developing the skills required for achieving grade A. The Argument Boosters provide knowledge and encourage the development of and confidence in application, analysis and evaluation skills; like the Concept Boosters, these have exam-style questions of increasing demand.

There is increasing interest in and use of SOLO taxonomy (Structure of Observed Learning Outcomes) in the UK. The Boosters aim to support relational and extended abstract stages of the SOLO taxonomy.

Problem Areas in Chemistry

Past examination papers and reports can be scrutinised to help understand the skills required to answer 'higher' examination questions. Understanding this can encourage learners to maximise their marks.

General problem areas

Written answers

- Often excessively verbose.

- Repeat the question with no answer.

- Make the same point more than once.

- Make contradicting statements.

- Do not pay attention to the stem of a question.

Data analysis

- Incorrect reading of graphs and charts.

- Mathematical weaknesses in calculations.

- Poor extrapolation of data.

- Limited ability to apply knowledge to a new situation.

- Incorrect application of concepts of reliability, accuracy and validity.

Specific problem areas

Knowledge and understanding

- Balancing chemical equations.

- Ionic bonding.

- Structures and formulae of hydrocarbons.

- Chemical formulae of common compounds.

- Electrolysis and half equations.

- Limestone cycle of reactions.

- History of the Periodic Table.

- Polymerisation.

Problem Areas in Chemistry

Application

- Renewable energy resources and finite fossil fuels.

- Earth science and prediction of earthquakes or volcanoes.

- The past and future atmosphere.

- The efficiency of the Haber process.

Exam Preparation Checklist

Months before

- [ ] Learn the keywords of each topic and their definitions: use Knowledge Boosters.
- [ ] Explain key concepts and learn them: use Concept Boosters.
- [ ] Explain the key experiments: use Experiment Boosters.
- [ ] Explain the key issues: use Argument Boosters.
- [ ] Make a summary revision sheet for each topic.
- [ ] Practise past exam questions regularly.
- [ ] Ask for help if you do not understand a specific area.

Weeks before

- [ ] Make sure you know when and where the exam is.
- [ ] Make sure you know which topics the exam covers.
- [ ] Go back to the exam specification and the text book to identify keywords, key concepts, key experiments and key issues.
- [ ] Make sure you can spell all keywords.

The day before

- [ ] Double check the time and location of the exam.
- [ ] Read through all your summary notes.
- [ ] Self-test on the areas you find difficult.
- [ ] Pack your exam kit: pencil, pen, ruler, calculator etc.
- [ ] Eat well and get an early night.

In the exam

- [ ] Read the question carefully – note the stem word of a question.
- [ ] If writing, write clearly.
- [ ] Do not waffle; write clearly and concisely.
- [ ] If you make a mistake, cross it out clearly and write the correct answer clearly.
- [ ] If you have time, read through all your answers.

I Can Get a Grade A* Checklist

If you can do most of these things, it is likely that you can achieve an A* grade in science examination papers.

General

- ☐ In a topic I can state the meanings of all keywords.
- ☐ In a topic I can spell all keywords.
- ☐ In a topic I can explain all key concepts.
- ☐ In a topic I can explain the key experiments or investigations.
- ☐ In a topic I can explain the main arguments of key issues.
- ☐ I can apply my knowledge and understanding to new situations.

Experiments and investigations

- ☐ I can plan, analyse and evaluate unfamiliar investigations.
- ☐ I can justify variables as independent, dependent and control.
- ☐ I can decide upon the aims, hypothesis or prediction.
- ☐ I can explain if an experiment is reliable and suggest improvements.
- ☐ I can explain if an experiment is accurate and suggest improvements.
- ☐ I can draw justified conclusions from charts and graphs based on scientific ideas.

Tables, graphs and numbers

- ☐ I can calculate an average.
- ☐ I can calculate percentages and percentage change.
- ☐ I can present numbers as percentages, ratios, fractions and probabilities.
- ☐ I can explain patterns or trends in data in a table, chart or graph.
- ☐ I can use decimal places and appropriate significant figures.

Arguments

- ☐ I can evaluate the advantages and disadvantages of a new technology.
- ☐ I can suggest and evaluate environmental arguments.
- ☐ I can suggest and evaluate economic arguments.
- ☐ I can suggest and evaluate social arguments.
- ☐ I can suggest and evaluate ethical arguments.
- ☐ I can suggest why some scientific theories took time to be accepted.
- ☐ I can justify my conclusions with evidence or scientific ideas.

Communication

- ☐ I can describe trends in data clearly (change, direction, and by how much).
- ☐ I can explain scientific ideas in a logical sequence.
- ☐ I can answer a question from the command word, for example describe, explain, discuss, apply, evaluate.
- ☐ I can write a relevant and clear answer to a question.
- ☐ I can write using correct grammar, punctuation and spelling.

Linking Activities to Examination Specifications

	AQA	EDEXCEL	OCR
Knowledge Booster 1: Chemicals and Reactions	C1.1.3 C3.4.1	C2.5	C1 & 2
Knowledge Booster 2: Chemicals and Formulae	C1.1.3	C2.6	C2 & 4
Knowledge Booster 3: Ionic Bonding	C2.1.1	C2.2	C4 b
Knowledge Booster 4: Hydrocarbon Diagrams	C1.4.1	C1.2 C3.5	C1
Knowledge Booster 5	Any	Any	Any
Concept Booster 1: Electrons at Electrodes	C2.7.1	C3.3	C6 a
Concept Booster 2: Polymers	C1.5.2	C1.3	C1 e
Concept Booster 3: The Periodic Table	C3.1.1–3.1.2	C2.1	C4
Concept Booster 4: Limestone Reactions	C1.2	C1.2	C2 b
Concept Booster 5	Any	Any	Any
Experiment Booster 1c: Explaining Experiments – Making Fertilisers	HSW	HSW	HSW
Experiment Booster 2a: Understanding Line Graphs – Extrapolation from Data	HSW	HSW	HSW
Experiment Booster 2b: Understanding Line Graphs – Rates of Reaction	HSW	HSW	HSW
Experiment Booster 2c: Calculating Empirical Formulae	C2.3.3	C2.6	C5 b
Experiment Booster 3: Key Calculations – Bond Energies	C2.5.1 not required	C2.5	C3 f
Experiment Booster 4a: Key Calculations – Understanding Moles	C3.4.1	C3.2	C5 a
Experiment Booster 4c: Key Calculations – Balancing Equations	C1.1.3	C2.6	C3 & 4
Experiment Booster 5: Understanding Graphs and Charts	Any	Any	Any
Argument Booster 1: Fuels Forever?	C1.4	C1.5	C1 b
Argument Booster 2: Volcano Predictions	C1.7	C1.1	C2
Argument Booster 3: Our Future Atmosphere	C1.7.2	C1.1	C1 c
Argument Booster 4: Haber Economy	C3.5.1	C3.4	C2 e
Argument Booster 5: Controversial Issues	Any	Any	Any

Chemistry Knowledge Boosters: Teacher Notes

Rationale

Confidence with the keywords in chemistry is essential to getting at least an A grade. Both the meaning of the word and the spelling of the word are important. Using activities to encourage the use of the keywords, their meaning and their spelling builds that confidence. These activities require the learner to decide on the keyword from the definition, or they can try defining the keywords themselves.

Activities

These activities all aim to engage learners with the keywords and their definitions, encouraging increased familiarity and confidence in these words. In addition, the activities encourage learners to ensure that they can spell these keywords.

Suggested approaches

- Begin with a starter activity to establish current understanding.

- Towards the end of the topic use the activities to consolidate, review or revise.

- Use the activities for independent study in class or as homework.

How to use the self-testers

These are designed so that the answers can be folded back. The learners then write their answers to the first 10 definitions. Stop, fold answers out and check them and their spellings. Give scores out of 10. Concentrate on learning the answers or spellings that were wrong.

At this point, it is best to move on to the next set of definitions. Go through the same process. Later, try the first set again and see if there is an improvement.

When supporting learners with this activity, concentrate on praising the improvement rather than the actual score out of 10.

How to use the diagrams

Labelling and defining the parts of diagrams are skills that will boost knowledge. Learners can be given unlabelled master copies to label or, alternatively, laminate the unlabelled master copies with the answer sheet on the reverse. Learners can use a non-permanent marker to label the diagrams and check answers. Wipe off and try again.

Extension activities

Self-testers

- Reverse the activity: look at the answers and write the definitions.

- Teachers make their own sets of questions or definitions and answers using the exam specification or, even better, learners make their own and swap with others.

Diagrams

Define each part of the diagram.

Chemistry Knowledge Booster 1: Chemicals and Reactions

Students that achieve an A* grade can:

- use a wide range of keywords.

- spell all keywords correctly.

- explain in detail what the keywords mean.

Note: some of these words go beyond some GCSE specifications.

How to use the self-test questions

1   Read through the questions and answers.

2   Fold back the answers.

3   Answer each question by saying the answer and writing it down.

4   Check your answers, then check your spellings.

5   Repeat until you get most of the answers and spellings correct.

Atoms and bonding	Answer
1 The sub particle that orbits the nucleus of an atom.	1 electron
2 A bond that shares electrons between two atoms.	2 covalent bond
3 A bond caused by attraction between two oppositely charged ions.	3 ionic bond
4 The energy levels at which electrons orbit an atomic nucleus.	4 electron shell
5 The sub particle that has no charge.	5 neutron
6 Atoms with the same number of protons but differing numbers of neutrons; different forms of a single element.	6 isotope
7 An atom that has lost or gained electrons.	7 ion
8 The number of protons in a nucleus.	8 atomic number
9 The number of sub particles in a nucleus.	9 atomic mass
10 The sub particle that has a charge of +1.	10 proton

Oil chemistry	Answer
1 The breaking up of polymers.	1 cracking
2 The joining up of monomers.	2 polymerisation
3 The process used to separate crude oil into useful substances.	3 fractional distillation
4 A mixture of hydrocarbons extracted from the Earth.	4 crude oil
5 A hydrocarbon with no double bonds.	5 saturated molecule
6 A hydrocarbon with double bonds.	6 unsaturated molecule
7 The ability to be broken down by sunlight and bacteria.	7 biodegradable
8 Materials that are often made by polymerisation.	8 plastics
9 A single molecular unit that can be joined into a polymer.	9 monomer
10 The solution used to test for alkenes.	10 bromine water

FOLD

Chemistry Knowledge Booster 1:
Chemicals and Reactions

Reactions	Answer
1 The breakdown of a molecule, often by heat.	1 decomposition
2 A reaction in which a particle gains electrons.	2 reduction
3 A reaction in which a particle loses electrons.	3 oxidation
4 A reaction between an acid and an alkali.	4 neutralisation
5 The reaction between a metal and a more reactive metal compound.	5 displacement
6 The substances that join together in a reaction.	6 reactants
7 The substances that are formed in a reaction.	7 products
8 A substance that increases the rate of reaction without reacting.	8 catalyst
9 Breaking up a substance using electricity.	9 electrolysis
10 A reaction that releases energy.	10 exothermic

Periodic Table	Answer
1 The horizontal rows in the Periodic Table.	1 period
2 The vertical columns in the Periodic Table.	2 group
3 The block of elements that consists of metals between Groups 2 and 3.	3 transition metals
4 Elements that are usually shiny and conduct electricity.	4 metals
5 The group of metals that react with water to form hydroxides.	5 alkali metals
6 The group of inert gases.	6 noble gases
7 The group of elements that exist in all different states, and that form salts.	7 halogens
8 The person responsible for the modern Periodic Table.	8 Mendeleev
9 The number of protons in an element.	9 atomic number
10 The reoccurring pattern of properties in elements in the Periodic Table.	10 periodicity

Chemical tests	Answer
1 Lit splint, squeaky pop.	1 hydrogen
2 Bleaches damp blue litmus paper.	2 chlorine gas
3 Cobalt chloride paper turns pink.	3 water vapour
4 Lime water goes cloudy.	4 carbon dioxide
5 Bromine water turns colourless.	5 alkenes
6 Lilac flame test.	6 potassium
7 Scarlet red flame test.	7 lithium
8 Pale blue precipitate forms with sodium hydroxide.	8 copper ions
9 Gas that turns damp red litmus paper blue.	9 ammonia
10 Sliver nitrate turns pale yellow.	10 iodide ions

FOLD

Students that achieve an A* grade can:

- use a wide range of keywords.

- spell all keywords correctly.

- explain simply what the keywords mean.

How to use the self-test questions

1   Read through the questions and answers.

2   Fold back the answers.

3   Answer each question by saying the answer and writing it down.

4   Check your answers, then check your spellings.

5   Repeat until you get most of the answers and spellings correct.

Carbon chemistry	Answer
1 A saturated hydrocarbon.	1 alkane
2 An unsaturated hydrocarbon.	2 alkene
3 Hydrocarbons with an OH group attached.	3 alcohols
4 Used as a perfume or flavour.	4 esters
5 A molecule that repels water.	5 hydrophobic
6 A molecule that attracts water.	6 hydrophilic
7 A substance that breaks up fats and oils.	7 emulsifier
8 Plant oils used to replace petrol.	8 biofuels
9 Plant oils that have been hardened using hydrogen.	9 margarine
10 A chain of C_{60} can form these.	10 nanotubes

Ion formulae	Answer
1 Hydrogen ion.	1 H^+
2 Hydroxide ion.	2 OH^-
3 Oxygen ion.	3 O^{2-}
4 Iron(III) ion. Fe^{2+} Fe^{3+}	4 Fe^{3+}
5 Aluminium ion.	5 Al^{3+}
6 Chloride ion.	6 Cl^-
7 Ammonium ion.	7 NH_4^+
8 Magnesium ion.	8 Mg^{2+}
9 Sulphate ion.	9 SO_4^{2-}
10 Carbonate ion.	10 CO_3^{2-}

FOLD

Chemistry Knowledge Booster 2: Chemicals and Formulae

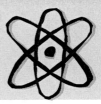

Common carbon molecules	Answer
1 Buckminsterfullerene.	1 C_{60}
2 The general formula for alkenes.	2 C_nH_{2n}
3 The general formula for alkanes.	3 C_nH_{2n+2}
4 Methane.	4 CH_4
5 Ethane.	5 C_2H_6
6 Propane.	6 C_3H_8
7 Ethene.	7 C_2H_4
8 Propene.	8 C_3H_6
9 Ethanol.	9 C_2H_5OH
10 Glucose.	10 $C_6H_{12}O_6$

Common compounds and state symbols	Answer
1 Water at room temperature and pressure.	1 H_2O (l)
2 Carbon dioxide at room temperature and pressure.	2 CO_2 (g)
3 Copper oxide at room temperature and pressure.	3 CuO (s)
4 Magnesium oxide at room temperature and pressure.	4 MgO (s)
5 Lithium hydroxide in solution at room temperature and pressure.	5 $LiOH$ (aq)
6 Dilute hydrochloric acid.	6 HCl (aq)
7 Steam.	7 H_2O (g)
8 Hydrogen ions in solution.	8 H^+ (aq)
9 Chloride ions in solution.	9 Cl^- (aq)
10 Ammonia at room temperature and pressure.	10 NH_3 (g)

Common compounds	Answer
1 Sulfuric acid.	1 H_2SO_4
2 Hydrochloric acid.	2 HCl
3 Sodium chloride.	3 $NaCl$
4 Sodium hydroxide	4 $NaOH$
5 Ammonia.	5 NH_3
6 Sodium carbonate.	6 Na_2CO_3
7 Sodium hydrogen carbonate.	7 $NaHCO_3$
8 Iron(III) hydroxide.	8 $Fe(OH)_3$
9 Iron(II) nitrate.	9 $Fe(NO_3)_2$
10 Hydrated copper sulfate.	10 $CuSO_4.5H_2O$

FOLD

Chemistry Knowledge Booster 3a:
Ionic Bonding

Students that achieve an A* grade can:

- use a wide range of diagrams.

- explain the difference between similar words and definitions.

How to use the diagrams

1   Draw the diagrams.

2   Check your answers against the answer sheet.

3   Repeat until you feel confident.

Ionic bonding: transferring electrons

Draw dot and cross diagrams for the following ions and ionic compounds. The first example is done for you.

Ionic compound	Metal atom(s)	Non-metal atom(s)	Ionic compound
Sodium chloride	Na[2,8,1]	Cl[2,8,7]	Na⁺[2,8]⁺ Cl⁻[2,8,8]⁻
Magnesium oxide			
Magnesium chloride			
Sodium oxide			

Chemistry Knowledge Booster 3b:
Ionic Bonding – Answers

Ionic compound	Metal atom(s)	Non-metal atom(s)	Ionic compound
Sodium chloride	Na[2,8,1]	Cl[2,8,7]	Na$^+$[2,8]$^+$ Cl$^-$[2,8,8]$^-$
Magnesium oxide	Mg[2,8,2]	O[2,6]	Mg^{2+}[2,8]$^{2+}$ O^{2-}[2,8]$^{-2}$
Magnesium chloride	Mg[2,8,2]	Cl[2,8,7]	Mg^{2+}[2,8]$^{2+}$ Cl$^-$[2,8,8]$^-$ Cl$^-$[2,8,8$^-$]$^-$
Sodium oxide	Na[2,8,1]	O[2,6]	Na$^+$[2,8]$^+$ Na$^+$[2,8,]$^+$ O^{2-}[2,8]$^{-2}$

22   © Badger Learning

Chemistry Knowledge Booster 4a: Hydrocarbon Diagrams

Students that achieve an A* grade can:

- represent a wide range of molecular structures.

- explain the difference between similar words and definitions.

How to use the diagrams

1 Try to draw the diagram correctly.

2 Check your answers against the answer sheet.

3 Repeat until you feel confident.

Molecule	Formula	Structure
Ethane		
Butane		
Ethene		
Propene		
Ethanol		
Tetrafluoroethene		

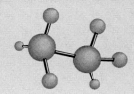

Molecule	Formula	Structure
Ethane	C_2H_6	
Butane	C_4H_{10}	
Ethene	C_2H_4	
Propene	C_3H_6	
Ethanol	C_2H_5OH	
Tetrafluoroethene	C_2F_4	

Chemistry Knowledge Booster 5:
Create a Knowledge Booster

Use your exam specification to write your own questions and answers. Use this sheet for revision and swap your questions with your friends.

Knowledge Booster Topic: _____	Answer

Knowledge Booster Topic: _____	Answer

Knowledge Booster Topic: _____	Answer

FOLD

Chemistry Concept Boosters

Rationale

Understanding key concepts in chemistry is essential for a learner to be able to explain processes and solve problems. Learners need to be able to understand and construct these concepts for themselves, identifying the important features, making links and being able to sequence an explanation. By engaging learners with some long-answer questions, they can try and improve their attempts. As they do more of these, their understanding will improve and their confidence will increase.

Activities

These activities aim to encourage learners to construct their own understanding of the key concepts. The activities are structured using key questions to answer, keywords to understand and statements to sequence. Once the concept has been tackled using the activity, learners can then apply their understanding to some long-answer questions. These are arranged with increasing demand: explain, apply and evaluate.

Suggested approaches

- Begin with a starter activity to establish current understanding.
- Towards the end of the topic use the activities to consolidate, review or revise.
- Use the activities for independent study in class or as homework.

Learners could be given the Concept Boosters as a homework activity, followed by a classroom activity of applying their knowledge and understanding to the long-answer questions or vice-versa.

Note that the sequencing activity has no definitive answer, but it has to be logical.

An example marking scheme (adapted from OCR Gateway mark schemes) is provided for the long-answer questions, but most of the points needed should be found in the Concept Boosters.

Extension activities

- Encourage learners to make their own Concept Boosters from a textbook or specification.
- Choose concepts that cover large parts of the specification.

Chemistry Concept Booster 1a:
Electrons at Electrodes

Students that achieve a grade A or above can explain key concepts and processes in detail. They can also use a range of keywords to explain concepts and processes.

When you first try these activities use a GCSE textbook or GCSE website to help you if you need it. Then, next time, try the activities without any help.

Questions

Write at least one paragraph to answer each of these questions.

1   What is electrolysis?

2   Why is electrolysis useful?

3   How can half equations be used to represent electrolysis?

4   Which types of substances can be separated using electrolysis?

Keywords

Make sure that you know the meanings of these keywords and how to use them.

- *electrode*
- *electrons*
- *electrolyte*
- *electrolysis*
- *reactivity*

- *electroplating*
- *extraction*
- *ions*
- *molten*
- *solution*

- *movement*
- *liquid*
- *half equation*
- *positive*
- *negative*

- *reduction*
- *oxidisation*
- *cathode*
- *anode*

Sequencing

Put these phrases about electrons at electrodes into a logical sequence.

A   When an electric current is passed through, the molten lead bromide ($PbBr_2$) breaks down.

B   The positively charged ions, Pb^{2+}, move to the negative electrode.

C   The negatively charged bromide ions, $2Br^-$, move to the positive electrode.

D   Here, the positive ions are reduced to make lead atoms: $Pb^{2+} + 2e^-$.

E   Here, the negative ions are oxidised to make bromine molecules: $2Br^- - 2e^-$

F   When lead bromide is melted, the Pb^{2+} and Br^- ions are free to move about within the liquid.

G   Lead bromide is the electrolyte.

H   Two electrodes are placed in the liquid lead bromide.

Next steps

Use Concept Booster 1b to apply your improved knowledge and understanding to long-answer exam questions.

Use Concept Booster 1a to help you practise answering questions. Students that achieve at least a grade A can:

- write a clear and detailed answer.

- use correct spelling, punctuation and grammar.

- write in an organised, logical sequence.

- use keywords and phrases accurately.

Question 1 (Explain)

Use half equations to explain how lead bromide is broken down by electrolysis. (6 marks)

....

....

....

....

....

Question 2 (Apply)

Explain how molten sodium chloride is broken down by electrolysis; use half equations to explain why each substance is produced at each electrode. (6 marks)

....

....

....

....

....

Question 3 (Evaluate)

Discuss what considerations you would take into account when using electrolysis to extract lead. (6 marks)

....

....

....

....

....

Chemistry Concept Booster 2a: Polymers

Students that achieve a grade A or above can explain key concepts and processes in detail. They can also use a range of keywords to explain concepts and processes.

When you first try these activities use a GCSE textbook or GCSE website to help you if you need it. Then, next time, try the activities without any help.

Questions

Write at least one paragraph to answer each of these questions.

1 What is a polymer?

2 Which hydrocarbons are suitable for polymerisation?

3 How is polythene made?

4 Why are plastics considered to be unfriendly to the environment?

Keywords

Make a mind map of these keywords to show how they are linked.

- monomer
- polymer
- polymerisation
- cracking
- condensation

- ethene
- propene
- styrene
- covalent
- double bond

- single bond addition
- hydrogen
- carbon
- chlorine

- plastics
- PVC
- polythene
- polypropene
- biodegradable

Sequencing

Put these phrases about making polythene into a logical sequence.

A Monomers are alkenes that can be joined together to make polymers.

B This causes one of the double bonds to 'open'.

C This makes a chain of ethene monomers become a polythene polymer.

D Many ethene monomers are heated and exposed to a catalyst.

E This is called addition polymerisation.

F This means that the carbon atoms from each monomer can join up.

G Ethene is an alkene; it contains a double bond between two carbon atoms.

Next steps

Use Concept Booster 2b to apply your improved knowledge and understanding to long-answer exam questions.

Chemistry Concept Booster 2b: Polymers Questions

Use Concept Booster 2a to help you practise answering questions. Students that achieve at least a grade A can:

- write a clear and detailed answer.
- use correct spelling, punctuation and grammar.
- write in an organised, logical sequence.
- use keywords and phrases accurately.

Question 1 (Explain)

Explain what polymerisation is in detail. (6 marks)

....

....

....

....

....

Question 2 (Apply)

Explain why polymerisation is an important industrial process. (6 marks)

....

....

....

....

....

Question 3 (Evaluate)

Discuss the future of plastics. Justify your conclusion. (6 marks)

....

....

....

....

....

Chemistry Concept Booster 3a:
The Periodic Table

Students that achieve a grade A or above can explain key concepts and processes in detail. They can also use a range of keywords to explain concepts and processes.

When you first try these activities use a GCSE textbook or GCSE website to help you if you need it. Then, next time, try the activities without any help.

Questions

Write at least one paragraph to answer each of these questions.

1 How is the modern Periodic Table organised?

2 What does the modern Periodic Table show?

3 Why was Mendeleev's contribution so important to making the Periodic Table?

4 What were the early attempts of organising the elements?

Keywords

Make a mind map of these keywords to show how they are linked.

- groups
- periods
- elements
- atomic mass
- prediction
- gaps
- atomic number
- proton
- electron
- Döbereiner
- Newlands
- Mendeleev

Sequencing

Put these phrases about the Periodic Table into a logical sequence.

A The new Periodic Table was used to predict the properties of undiscovered elements.

B John Newlands put all the elements in order of their mass.

C He found some patterns, but lots of elements did not fit.

D The modern Periodic Table is arranged in order of atomic number.

E It was assumed that some elements had not yet been discovered.

F Dmitri Mendeleev put the elements in order of mass, but left gaps.

G First attempts to order the elements failed because some substances were compounds.

Next steps

Use Concept Booster 3b to apply your improved knowledge and understanding to long-answer exam questions.

H

1

HYDROGEN

1

Use Concept Booster 3a to help you practise answering questions. Students that achieve at least a grade A can:

- write a clear and detailed answer.

- use correct spelling, punctuation and grammar.

- write in an organised, logical sequence.

- use keywords and phrases accurately.

Question 1 (Explain)

Explain how scientists first attempted to classify the elements. (6 marks)

....

....

....

....

....

Question 2 (Apply)

Explain how the modern Periodic Table is used by scientists now. (6 marks)

....

....

....

....

....

Question 3 (Synthesis)

Explain the assumptions that Mendeleev made when ordering the elements and how these contributed to his success in making the Periodic Table. (6 marks)

....

....

....

....

....

Chemistry Concept Booster 4a: Limestone Reactions

Students that achieve a grade A or above can explain key concepts and processes in detail. They can also use a range of keywords to explain concepts and processes.

When you first try these activities use a GCSE textbook or GCSE website to help you if you need it. Then, next time, try the activities without any help.

Questions

Write at least one paragraph to answer each of these questions.

1   What are the uses of limestone?

2   How is limestone formed?

3   What are the problems with quarrying limestone?

4   What are the reactions involved in making limestone useful?

Keywords

Make a mind map of these keywords to show how they are linked.

- limestone
- fossilisation
- sedimentary
- quarry
- glass

- paper
- steel
- calcium hydroxide
- calcium oxide

- calcium hydroxide solution
- calcium carbonate
- carbon dioxide
- thermal decomposition

- quicklime
- slaked lime
- lime water
- cement
- concrete

Sequencing

Put these phrases about limestone reactions into a logical sequence.

A   Limestone is calcium carbonate.

B   If a small amount of water is added to quicklime, it makes calcium hydroxide.

C   If this is added to more water and filtered, it produces lime water.

D $Ca(OH)_2$ (aq) + CO_2 (g) $\rightarrow$ $CaCO_3$ (s) + H_2O (l)

E CaO (s) + H_2O (l) $\rightarrow$ $Ca(OH)_2$ (s)

F $CaCO_3$ (s) $\rightarrow$ CaO (s) + CO_2 (g)

G   Calcium carbonate can be produced by adding carbon dioxide.

Next steps

Use Concept Booster 4b to apply your improved knowledge and understanding to long-answer exam questions.

Chemistry Concept Booster 4b: Limestone Reactions Questions

Use Concept Booster 4a to help you practise answering questions. Students that achieve at least a grade A can:

- write a clear and detailed answer.
- use correct spelling, punctuation and grammar.
- write in an organised, logical sequence.
- use keywords and phrases accurately.

Question 1 (Explain)

Use chemical equations to explain how the limestone reactions form a cycle. (6 marks)

....

....

....

....

....

Question 2 (Apply)

Explain which of the limestone reactions contribute to the greenhouse effect; include symbol equations. (6 marks)

....

....

....

....

....

Question 3 (Evaluate)

Discuss the benefits and problems of quarrying for limestone. (6 marks)

....

....

....

....

....

© Badger Learning

Topic: _____

Make your own Concept Booster by using a specification, a GCSE textbook or GCSE website to help you if you need it. Use it for revision.

Students that achieve a grade A or above can explain key concepts and processes. They can also explain their ideas logically.

Questions

Write four key questions.

1 ....

2 ....

3 ....

4 ....

Keywords

Identify the keywords and put them into a mind map.

- ....
- ....
- ....
- ....
- ....
- ....
- ....
- ....

Sequencing

Write an explanation with phrases in a logical sequence.

A ....

B ....

C ....

D ....

E ....

F ....

G ....

H ....

Chemistry Concept Booster 5b: Suggested Mark Criteria Grid for Long-answer Questions

Use this mark grid, adapted from an examiner's mark scheme, to give yourself a mark for your answers.

5–6 Marks

- ☐ Answers the question from the command word, for example explain, analyse or discuss.
- ☐ All key points are given in detail.
- ☐ All information in answer is relevant and clear.
- ☐ All information is organised and presented in a logical way.
- ☐ Keywords or phrases are used appropriately.
- ☐ Few, if any, errors in grammar, punctuation and spelling.

3–4 Marks

- ☐ Answers the question from the command word, for example explain, analyse or discuss.
- ☐ Most key points are mentioned; one or two may be missing.
- ☐ Most information in answer is relevant and clear.
- ☐ Most information is organised and presented in a logical way.
- ☐ Most keywords or phrases are used appropriately.
- ☐ There are occasional errors in grammar, punctuation and spelling.

1–2 Marks

- ☐ Answers the question from the command word, for example describe, explain or discuss.
- ☐ One or two key points are mentioned.
- ☐ Answer is unclear or irrelevant information is provided.
- ☐ Most information is **not** organised and presented in a logical way.
- ☐ Limited use of the keywords and phrases.
- ☐ There are several errors in grammar, punctuation and spelling.

0 Marks

- ☐ Ignores command word
- ☐ Insufficient or irrelevant science.

What will you do to improve next time?

Chemistry Experiment Boosters: Teacher Notes

Rationale

Understanding experimental design and scientific methods in chemistry is essential for a learner to be able to think scientifically. Learners need to be able to identify features of experiments that are strengths or limitations, interpret data and use evidence to make conclusions.

Activities

These activities aim to encourage learners to apply their understanding of scientific method to a range of activities to help them gain confidence in areas that often cause learners problems. These focus on understanding experiments, analysing charts and graphs and, finally, some key calculations that are often troublesome for learners. These are designed to stretch the more-able learner and provide unfamiliar situations in which to apply scientific knowledge and understanding.

Suggested approaches

There are three types of task: explaining experiments, understanding graphs and charts, and key calculations.

Explaining experiments

Experiment Booster 1a can be used for any experiment that is described. Experiment Booster 1b has hints to help learners know what to look for. These can be used with Experiment Booster 1c (focus on making fertilisers). The 1a and 1b scaffolds can be applied to analyse any experimental design.

Understanding graphs and charts

Experiment Booster 5 can be used for any chart or graph as a scaffold to understand it. Examples include line graphs in Experiment Boosters 2a and 2b. Experiment Booster 2c focuses on calculating empirical formulae.

Key calculations

Experiment Booster 3a has a special focus on calculating bond energies. Answers for learners are provided on Experiment Booster 3b.

Experiment Booster 4a concentrates on moles and using moles formulae; answers are provided on Experiment Booster 4b. Finally, a task on balancing equations in chemistry is the focus of Experiment Booster 4c.

Extension activities

Try a variety of past exam questions using Experiment Booster 1a: Explaining Experiments

Chemistry Experiment Booster 1a: Explaining Experiments

Students that achieve a grade A or above can:

- identify variables: independent, dependent and control.

- make a hypothesis or prediction.

- understand reliability, accuracy and precision.

- suggest relevant improvements to an experiment.

To help you understand experiments, use this table to identify the features of an experiment. For some sections the information may not be available. These can be used to help identify improvements.

List all the variables in the experiment:		
The independent variable:	**The dependent variable:**	
The aim, hypothesis or prediction:		
Is there a control? If so, what is it and why is it used?		
Comment on the reliability:	**Comment on the accuracy:**	**Comment on the precision:**
The experiment could be improved by:		

Chemistry Experiment Booster 1b: Explaining Experiments Support Sheet

This sheet will help you to complete Experiment Booster 1a if you get stuck.

List all the variables in the experiment:
Variables are the factors that could affect the investigation or experiment, for example time, temperature, pH, mass, length.

The independent variable:
The variable that is being investigated.
The variable that the experimenter changes.

The dependent variable:
The variable that is measured or observed.
The variable that the experimenter finds out.

The aim, hypothesis or prediction:
What is the experiment trying to find out?
What is expected to happen and why?

Is there a control? If so, what is it and why is it used?
A control is used to check that only one variable is having the effect, for example in medical trials a placebo is used to ensure that any changes are the result of the actual active ingredient and not just the psychological effect of taking a tablet.

Comment on the reliability:
How many times was the experiment repeated?
The more times, the more reliable.

Comment on the accuracy:
How close is the measurement to the true value?
What equipment was used to make measurements?
Electronic measurements are more accurate than measurements made by humans.

Comment on the precision:
Was the data precise enough to form a valid conclusion?
Were the readings close enough together?
Does the data tell you what you wanted to know?

The experiment could be improved by:
Think about the methods and apparatus used. Could it be better? How?
Are the results reliable? Could it benefit from being repeated?
Are the results accurate? Could better measurements be taken? How?
Are the results precise? Could it benefit from more measurements, are they close enough together, does the data tell you what the experiment was looking for?

Chemistry Experiment Booster 1c: Explaining Experiments – Making Fertilisers

Use Experiment Booster 1a to help you understand this experiment.

Making fertilisers

Describe how you would make the fertiliser ammonium phosphate through the reaction of an acid with an alkali. Include:

- The names of the apparatus and techniques you would use.
- The names of the reactants.
- Your experimental method.
- How a neutral solution is obtained.
- How solid fertiliser is obtained.
- Balanced symbol equations.

Write in full sentences, in a logical order, and using correct punctuation and grammar.

....
....
....
....
....
....
....
....
....
....
....
....
....
....
....
....
....
....
....
....

Chemistry Experiment Booster 2a: Understanding Line Graphs – Extrapolation from Data

Students that achieve a grade A or above can:

- extrapolate data.

- take accurate readings from graphs.

Use Experiment Booster 5 to understand the graph, then answer the questions underneath the graph.

Two students burnt magnesium ribbon in a crucible and measured the mass of magnesium oxide that was left. The results are in the graph.

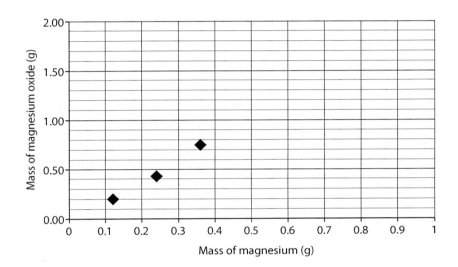

Questions

1   Write the word equation for this reaction.

2   Write the balanced symbol equation for this reaction.

3   Extrapolate the graph to estimate the mass of magnesium oxide produced when burning 1 gram of magnesium ribbon.

4   Discuss the accuracy of using extrapolation in this way. Suggest improvements.

Students that achieve a grade A or above can:

- analyse line graphs.

- describe trends or relationships between variables.

- apply scientific knowledge and understanding to make suggestions and conclusions.

Use Experiment Booster 5 to understand the graph, then answer the questions underneath the graph.

This graph shows the volume of carbon dioxide produced when reacting calcium carbonate chips with hydrochloric acid at 20°C.

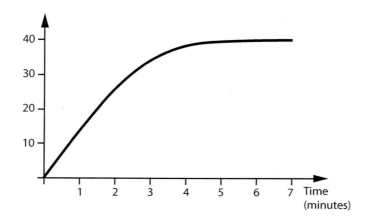

Questions

1   Suggest the label and units for the y axis.

2   Suggest three ways to increase the rate of reaction.

3   Calculate the rate of reaction at three minutes.

4   Explain each part of the graph by describing the behaviour of particles.

5   Draw another line on the graph to show the reaction at 10°C. Justify your new line.

Chemistry Experiment Booster 2c: Calculating Empirical Formulae

Students that achieve a grade A or above can calculate empirical formulae.

Atomic mass (Ar) of elements

Mg	O	S	N	H
24	16	32	14	1

Worked example

2.4g of magnesium reacts with 1.6g of oxygen to form an oxide. What is the formula of this oxide?

	Mg	O
1. Write the word equation:	magnesium + oxygen → magnesium oxide	
2. Identify the mass of each element	2.4	1.6
3. Find the atomic mass (Ar) of each element	24	16
4. Divide the mass by the atomic mass	2.4 ÷ 24 = 0.1	1.6 ÷ 16 = 0.1
5. Derive the ratio	1	1
6. Apply to the formula	MgO	

Chemistry Experiment Booster 2c: Calculating Empirical Formulae

Question 1

3.2g of sulfur reacts with oxygen to produce 6.4g of a sulfur oxide. What is the formula of the sulfur oxide?

	S	O
1. Write the word equation:		
2. Identify the mass of each element *Note: you need to work this out for oxygen!*		
3. Find the atomic mass (Ar) of each element		
4. Divide the mass by the atomic mass		
5. Derive the ratio		
6. Apply to the formula		

Question 2

280 tonnes of nitrogen reacts with hydrogen to produce 340 tonnes of ammonia. What is the formula of ammonia?

	N	H
1. Write the word equation:		
2. Identify the mass of each element		
3. Find the atomic mass (Ar) of each element		
4. Divide the mass by the atomic mass		
5. Derive the ratio		
6. Apply to the formula		

Students that achieve a grade A or above can:

- use equations to solve problems.

- present answers to an appropriate number of decimal places.

- show the steps in their calculation.

Calculating ΔH

Use energy level diagrams to work out the energy change (ΔH) of a reaction:

- Breaking bonds requires energy (endothermic).

- Making bonds gives out energy (exothermic).

Bonds and average bond energies

Bond	Bond energy kJ/mol
H–H	436
Cl–Cl	243
H–Cl	432
H–Br	366
O=O	498
Br–Br	193
O–H	464

Worked example

Reaction between hydrogen and chlorine.

Step 1. Write the balanced symbol equation. $H_2 + Cl_2 \rightarrow 2HCl$
Step 2. Calculate the energy needed to **break** all the bonds. H–H + Cl–Cl 436 + 243 = 679 kJ/mol
Step 3. Calculate the energy needed to **make** the new bonds. 2 × H–Cl 2 × 432 = 864 kJ/mol
Step 4. Calculate the energy change. breaking – making = energy change (ΔH) 679 – 864 = **–185 kJ/mol**
There is energy left over from the reaction (it is a minus figure), therefore the reaction is **exothermic**.

Chemistry Experiment Booster 3a:
Key Calculations – Bond Energies

Question 1

The decomposition of hydrogen bromide into hydrogen and bromine.

Step 1.
Step 2.
Step 3.
Step 4.

Question 2

Hydrogen burning in air to form steam.

Step 1.
Step 2.
Step 3.
Step 4.

Question 1

The decomposition of hydrogen bromide into hydrogen and bromine.

Step 1. $2HBr \rightarrow H_2 + Br_2$
Step 2. Breaking = $2 \times$ H$-$Br = 2×366 = 732 kJ/mol
Step 3. Making = H$-$H + Br$-$Br = 436 + 193 = 629 kJ/mol
Step 4. breaking – making = 732 – 629 = +103 kJ/mol
Positive ΔH $\therefore$ endothermic

Question 2

Hydrogen burning in air to form steam.

Step 1. $2H_2 + O_2 \rightarrow 2H_2O$
Step 2. Breaking = $(2 \times$ H–H$)$ + O=O = (2×436) + 498 = 1370 kJ/mol
Step 3. Making = $4 \times$ H$-$O = 4×464 = 1856 kJ/mol
Step 4. breaking – making = 1370 – 1856 = –486 kJ/mol
Negative ΔH $\therefore$ exothermic

Chemistry Experiment Booster 4a:
Key Calculations – Understanding Moles

Students that achieve a grade A or above can:

- apply the concept of moles to a range of situations.
- calculate using moles formulae.

Key equations

$$\frac{mass}{Ar} = \text{moles of atoms}$$

$$\frac{\text{volume of gas } (dm^3)}{24} = \text{moles of gas}$$

$$\text{moles in solution} = \text{concentration} \times \frac{\text{volume of solution } (cm^3)}{1000}$$

Ar or RAM of some elements

H	C	O	N	F	Cl	Na
1	12	16	14	19	35.5	23

Question 1

1   How many moles of atoms are there in 3.6g of carbon?

   ....

2   How many moles of atoms are there in 1.6g of oxygen?

   ....

3   How many moles of atoms are there in 140g of nitrogen?

   ....

Question 2

1   What is the mass of 10 moles of fluorine atoms?

   ....

2   What is the mass of 20 moles of hydrogen atoms?

   ....

3   What is the mass of 0.5 moles of carbon?

   ....

Chemistry Experiment Booster 4a: Key Calculations – Understanding Moles

Question 3

   1   How many moles of gas molecules are there in $24dm^3$ of hydrogen gas?

       ....

   2   How many moles of gas molecules are there in $6dm^3$ of oxyger gas?

       ....

   3   How many moles of gas molecules are there in $48cm^3$ of methane gas?

       ....

Question 4

At standard room temperature and pressure:

   1   What is the volume of 0.1 mole of hydrogen gas?

       ....

   2   What is the volume of 2 moles of oxygen gas?

       ....

   3   What is the volume of 6 moles of carbon dioxide gas?

       ....

Question 5

   1   How many moles are in $500cm^3$ of $2 \ mol/dm^3$ hydrochloric acid?

       ....

   2   How many moles are in $250cm^3$ of $1 \ mol/dm^3$ sodium hydroxide?

       ....

   3   How many moles are in $50cm^3$ of $0.5 \ mol/dm^3$ sodium chloride?

       ....

Question 1

1   How many moles of atoms are there in 3.6g of carbon? 3.6 ÷ 12 = 0.3 moles

2   How many moles of atoms are there in 1.6g of oxygen? 1.6 ÷ 16 = 0.1 moles

3   How many moles of atoms are there in 140g of nitrogen? 140 ÷ 14 = 10 moles

Question 2

1   What is the mass of 10 moles of fluorine atoms? 10 × 19 = 190g

2   What is the mass of 20 moles of hydrogen atoms? 20 × 1 = 20g

3   What is the mass of 0.5 moles of carbon? 0.5 × 12 = 6g

Question 3

1   How many moles of gas molecules are there in 24dm^3 of hydrogen gas?
     24dm^3 ÷ 24 = 1 mole of hydrogen gas

2   How many moles of gas molecules are there in 6dm^3 of oxygen gas?
     6dm^3 ÷ 24 = 0.25 moles of oxygen gas

3   How many moles of gas molecules are there in 48cm^3 of methane gas?
     48cm^3 ÷ 24,000 = 0.002 mole of methane gas

Question 4

At standard room temperature and pressure:

1   What is the volume of 0.1 mole of hydrogen gas? 0.1 × 24 = 2.4dm^3

2   What is the volume of 2 moles of oxygen gas? 2 × 24 = 48dm^3

3   What is the volume of 6 moles of carbon dioxide gas? 6 × 24 = 144dm^3

Question 5

1   How many moles are in 500cm^3 of 2 mol/dm^3 hydrochloric acid?

$$2 \times \frac{500}{1000} = 1 \text{ mole}$$

2   How many moles are in 250cm^3 of 1 mol/dm^3 sodium hydroxide?

$$1 \times \frac{250}{1000} = 0.25 \text{ mole}$$

3   How many moles are in 50cm^3 of 0.5 mol/dm^3 sodium chloride?

$$0.5 \times \frac{50}{1000} = 0.025 \text{ mole}$$

Chemistry Experiment Booster 4c:
Key Calculations – Balancing Equations

Students that achieve a grade A or above can:

- balance a wide range of chemical equations.
- use state symbols.

For each of the situations below, balance the equations and add state symbols.

1. $H_2 + O_2 \rightarrow H_2O$	
2. $CH_4 + O_2 \rightarrow H_2O + CO_2$	
3. $CO + NO \rightarrow N_2 + CO_2$	
4. $CaCO_3 \rightarrow CaO + CC_2$	
5. $N_2 + H_2 \rightleftharpoons NH_3$	
6. $Na + H_2O \rightarrow NaOH + H_2$	
7. $HCl + NaOH \rightarrow NaCl + H_2O$	
8. $Fe + Cl_2 \rightarrow FeCl_3$	
9. $NaHCO_3 \rightarrow Na_2CO_3 + CO_2 + H_2O$	
10. $C_6H_{12}O_6 \rightarrow CO_2 + C_2H_5OH$	

Students that achieve a grade A or above can:

- balance a wide range of chemical equations.
- use state symbols.

For each of the situations below, balance the equations and add state symbols.

1. $H_2 + O_2 \rightarrow H_2O$	1. $\mathbf{2}H_2 + O_2 \rightarrow \mathbf{2}H_2O$
2. $CH_4 + O_2 \rightarrow H_2O + CO_2$	2. $CH_4 + \mathbf{2}O_2 \rightarrow \mathbf{2}H_2O + CO_2$
3. $CO + NO \rightarrow N_2 + CO_2$	3. $\mathbf{2}CO + \mathbf{2}NO \rightarrow N_2 + \mathbf{2}CO_2$
4. $CaCO_3 \rightarrow CaO + CO_2$	4. $CaCO_3 \rightarrow CaO + CO_2$ (Note – no balancing required)
5. $N_2 + H_2 \rightleftharpoons NH_3$	5. $N_2 + \mathbf{3}H_2 \rightleftharpoons \mathbf{2}NH_3$
6. $Na + H_2O \rightarrow NaOH + H_2$	6. $\mathbf{2}Na + \mathbf{2}H_2O \rightarrow \mathbf{2}NaOH + H_2$
7. $HCl + NaOH \rightarrow NaCl + H_2O$	7. $HCl + NaOH \rightarrow NaCl + H_2O$ (Note – no balancing required)
8. $Fe + Cl_2 \rightarrow FeCl_3$	8. $\mathbf{2}Fe + \mathbf{3}Cl_2 \rightarrow \mathbf{2}FeCl_3$
9. $NaHCO_3 \rightarrow Na_2CO_3 + CO_2 + H_2O$	9. $\mathbf{2}NaHCO_3 \rightarrow Na_2CO_3 + CO_2 + H_2O$
10. $C_6H_{12}O_6 \rightarrow CO_2 + C_2H_5OH$	10. $C_6H_{12}O_6 \rightarrow \mathbf{2}CO_2 + \mathbf{2}C_2H_5OH$

Chemistry Experiment Booster 5: Understanding Graphs and Charts

Students that achieve a grade A or above can:

- analyse bar charts, histograms, pie charts and line graphs.

- describe trends or relationships between variables.

- take accurate readings from graphs.

This task will help you to improve these skills.

What type of graph or chart is it?	**Identify the independent variable(s):**
☐ A table of results ☐ Bar chart ☐ Histogram ☐ Pie chart ☐ Line graph ☐ Other	**Identify the dependent variable(s):**

What does the graph show?

What are the relationships or trends between the variables (if any)?

Are there any anomalous results? Explain them.	**How close together are the measurements? State the intervals.** **Could these be improved?**

What conclusions can be made from the evidence in the graph or chart?

Chemistry Argument Boosters: Teacher Notes

Rationale

Learners need to be able to understand controversial issues and be able to present an argument. These activities encourage learners to present different views and use evidence to make a decision.

Activities

These activities aim to encourage learners to use information to consider the advantages and disadvantages of technologies; develop arguments from a social, economic, environmental or ethical viewpoint; and discuss a controversial issue. Argument Booster 5 can be applied to most controversial issues and can be used as a scaffold to identify the key features of a debate.

Suggested approaches

These can be used as a starter activity to establish current understanding, towards the end of a topic to consolidate, review or revise, or for independent study in class or as a homework activity.

Argument Booster 5 should be used as the scaffold when reading information on the main Argument Boosters; the exam-style questions can then be used to apply this information.

Follow up with past exam questions.

Extension activities

Encourage learners to develop a summary of each controversial issue for revision.

Chemistry Argument Booster 1a: Fuels Forever?

Students that achieve a grade A or above can:

- apply scientific knowledge and understanding to new situations.

- evaluate different types of argument.

- justify a conclusion based on a particular viewpoint.

Use Argument Booster 5 to help you understand the issues.

Background information

Read this short report for information, then complete Argument Booster 1b.

Fossil fuels facts!

Fossil fuels formed over 400 million years ago. The large deposits are deep underground and are used mainly for fuels and manufacturing plastics.

If we use fossil fuels at the current rates:

- Natural gas reserves are estimated to last about 50 years.

- Oil reserves are estimated to last between 15 and 50 years.

- Coal reserves are expected to last over 1000 years; however, they will be under more demand as natural gas and oil become scarce.

The main issue with burning fossil fuels for energy is that they produce greenhouse gases that contribute to climate change.

As coal, oil and gas reserves are used up, they become more difficult to extract, and therefore more expensive.

Uranium and plutonium are also used in power stations, though these are non-renewable. It's thought that we have enough reserves of these to last about 80 years. Radioactive waste storage and decommissioning of nuclear power plants is very expensive however.

Future fuels

There are alternative renewable energy resources. These include wind, wave, solar and tidal power. Once these are set up, the energy supply is free and will continue forever.

They each have their own controversial issues however; for example, there are few places that are constantly windy.

The early research and design of machinery to capture these alternative resources is often expensive but, once they are up and running and can be mass produced, the cost falls.

Chemistry Arguments Booster 1b: Fuels Forever? Questions

Students that achieve a grade A or above can:

- apply scientific knowledge and understanding to new situations.

- evaluate different types of argument.

- justify a conclusion based on a particular viewpoint.

Question 1 (Explain)

Explain why fossil fuels cannot be used forever. (6 marks)

....

....

....

....

....

Question 2 (Evaluate)

Evaluate the economic arguments for reducing the use of fossil fuels. (6 marks)

....

....

....

....

....

Question 3 (Discuss)

Discuss whether people should reduce fossil fuel use now or wait until they run out. Justify your conclusion. (6 marks)

....

....

....

....

....

© Badger Learning

Chemistry Argument Booster 2a: Volcano Predictions

Students that achieve a grade A or above can:

- apply knowledge and understanding to unfamiliar situations.

- evaluate different types of argument.

- justify a conclusion based on a particular viewpoint.

Use Argument Booster 5 to help you understand the issues.

Background information

Read this short report for information, then complete Argument Booster 2b.

Predicting volcanoes

Volcanic eruptions can be dramatic and devastating to the communities that live near them, as well as to the surrounding areas and aircraft, which can be affected by ash clouds and irregular weather patterns. It is essential to be able to protect people and, where possible, infrastructure, by being able to predict when a volcano will erupt.

No two volcanoes are the same. Some are active and rarely erupt while others seem dormant and suddenly erupt with little warning. In addition, some volcanoes are more important to monitor because they are very close to human populations, whereas others would not affect many people if they blow.

Different countries have different ways of monitoring volcanic activity. Due to the variation between the technology of the countries and the importance of monitoring particular volcanoes, there is no internationally recognised way of monitoring volcanoes. However, the aviation industry does have a system that they use to alert pilots.

Warning about volcanic eruptions is not straightforward. If a volcano becomes more active, it still may not erupt. When should scientists recommend to local communities that they should evacuate their towns or cities? It is expensive to move lots of people quickly; it causes panic and disruption. Alternatively, sending a warning could save lives by moving the population away.

Students that achieve a grade A or above can:

- apply knowledge and understanding to unfamiliar situations.
- evaluate different types of argument.
- justify a conclusion based on a particular viewpoint.

Question 1 (Explain)

Explain why geologists cannot predict volcanic eruptions with 100% certainty. (6 marks)

....

....

....

....

....

Question 2 (Evaluate)

Write an argument using the social reasons for researching volcano predictions. (6 marks)

....

....

....

....

....

Question 3 (Discuss)

Discuss the economic reasons for investing in technology to predict volcanic eruptions. Justify your conclusion. (6 marks)

....

....

....

....

....

Chemistry Argument Booster 3a: Our Future Atmosphere

Students that achieve a grade A or above can:

- apply scientific knowledge to unfamiliar situations.

- justify a conclusion based on scientific knowledge and understanding.

Use Argument Booster 5 to help you understand the issues.

Background information

Read this short report for information, then complete Argument Booster 3b.

Mars: Earth II?

Earth's atmosphere has evolved over millions of years. From a steamy soup of methane, sulfur dioxide and ammonia, to plants evolving and producing oxygen, ozone being formed which protected life from harmful UV rays, carbon dioxide levels decreasing as fossils formed and oceans deepened, until the present day where nitrogen rules and oxygen and carbon dioxide have been in balance.

Now the Earth faces an uncertain future. Human activity has caused the level of carbon dioxide to increase more rapidly than ever before. This is causing climate change, rapid heating of the Earth's atmosphere and possibly unknown changes to the Earth's ability to support life. It could be that the Earth will become uninhabitable and humans need to find somewhere else to live.

The planet Venus is most like Earth in shape, but it is so near the Sun that surface temperatures make it uninhabitable. The next best place is Mars. It is a similar size, has confirmed sources of water and has iron-rich soil; however, it has little atmosphere and a very low temperature. Some scientists think that humans could colonise Mars by terraforming.

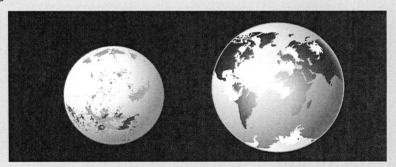

Terraforming would involve astronauts travelling for six months to get to Mars and building large dome structures that the astronauts could pressurise, producing an earth-like atmosphere and growing plants for food and oxygen. Once this early colony was established, more groups and equipment could be flown out to Mars. Large factories that produce carbon dioxide could be built to create a new atmosphere on Mars, causing the temperature to increase and an atmosphere to form that is similar to Earth's.

Students that achieve a grade A or above can:

- apply scientific knowledge to unfamiliar situations.

- justify a conclusion based on scientific knowledge and understanding.

Question 1 (Describe)

Describe the processes that can alter the chemical composition of the atmosphere. (6 marks)

....

....

....

....

....

Question 2 (Explain)

Explain the effects of human activity on the composition of the atmosphere. (6 marks)

....

....

....

....

....

Question 3 (Discuss)

Discuss whether Mars ever might have an atmosphere like Earth in the future. Justify your conclusion. (6 marks)

....

....

....

....

....

Students that achieve a grade A or above can:

- apply knowledge and understanding to unfamiliar situations.

- evaluate different types of argument.

- justify a conclusion based on a particular viewpoint.

Use Argument Booster 5 to help you understand the issues.

Background information

Read this information about the Haber process, then complete Argument Booster 4b.

The Haber process

The Haber process reacts nitrogen and hydrogen together to make ammonia. Ammonia is used in the production of artificial fertilisers.

$$nitrogen + hydrogen \rightleftharpoons ammonia$$

$$N_2 (g) + 3H_2 (g) \rightleftharpoons 2NH_3 (g)$$

The diagram below represents the Haber process.

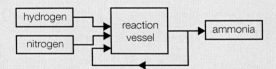

Hydrogen is made by reacting natural gas with steam, while nitrogen gas is condensed from the air. The steam is also used to generate high pressures.

The heat from exothermic reactions is used to heat the reaction vessel. Unreacted hydrogen and nitrogen are recycled back into the reaction vessel.

The conditions for making ammonia are carefully controlled. The higher the pressure, the more ammonia is produced. However, the higher the pressure, the stronger and more expensive the reaction vessel has to be. A pressure of between 150 and 300 atmospheres is used in the reaction vessel.

The higher the temperature, the more ammonia is produced. However, heating the vessel is expensive, so using the lowest temperature possible can save money. At equilibrium, ammonia of between 10% and 15% is produced between temperatures of 400°C and 450°C.

Under these optimum conditions, 15% ammonia is in the equilibrium mixture. This is drawn off. The remaining nitrogen and hydrogen are recycled.

Chemistry Argument Booster 4b: Haber Economy Questions

Students that achieve a grade A or above can:

- apply knowledge and understanding to unfamiliar situations.
- evaluate different types of argument.
- justify a conclusion based on a particular viewpoint.

Question 1 (Explain)

Explain the importance of the Haber process for society. (6 marks))

....

....

....

....

....

Question 2 (Explain)

Explain how chemists have made the Haber process as efficient as possible. (6 marks)

....

....

....

....

....

Question 3 (Discuss)

Discuss which are the most important factors in determining the cost of producing fertilisers using the Haber process. Justify your answer. (6 marks)

....

....

....

....

....

Chemistry Argument Booster 5: Controversial Issues

Topic area: _____

Fill in as much information as you can; you may not have enough for all the boxes.

What is the controversial issue?	
What are the advantages?	**What are the disadvantages?**
Environmental arguments:	**Economic arguments:**
Social arguments:	**Ethical and religious issues:**
Opinions:	**Facts or evidence:**
Your view/thoughts:	

Anderson, L.W., Krathwohl, D.R., Airasian, P.W., & Samuel, B. (2001). *A taxonomy for learning, teaching and assessing: A revision of Bloom's taxonomy of educational objectives*. New York: Longman.

Biggs, J., & Collis, K. (1982). *Evaluating the quality of learning: The SOLO taxonomy*. New York: Academic Press.

www.carboncounted.co.uk/when-will-fossil-fuels-run-out.html

www.pbs.org/exploringspace/mars/terraforming/page1.html

www.sciencemuseum.org.uk/ClimateChanging

www.wovo.org